AUDIO ENGINEERING

AND THE Science of Sound Waves

T2-AJT-344

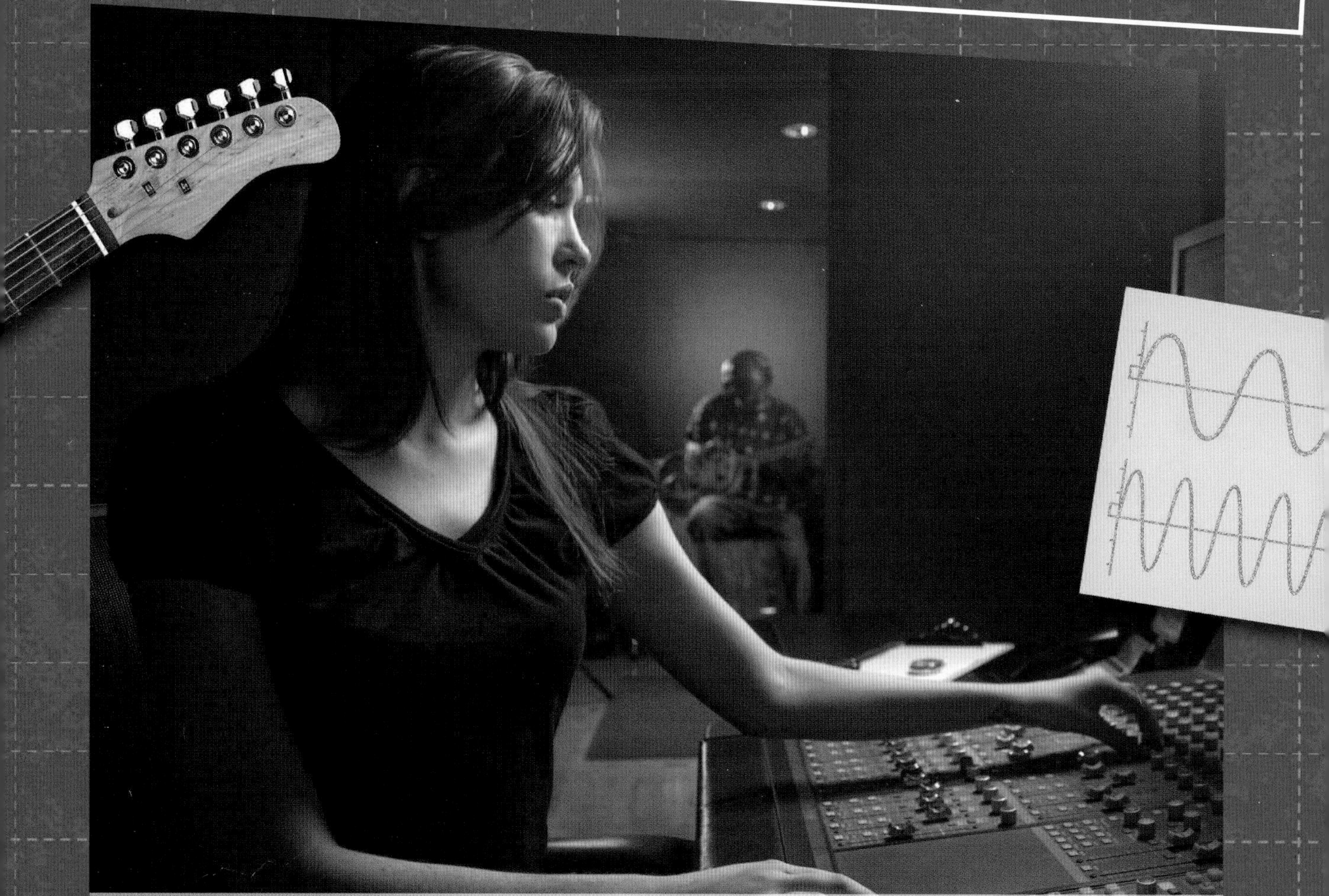

Crabtree Publishing Company

www.crabtreebooks.com

Anne Rooney

Crabtree Publishing Company
www.crabtreebooks.com

Author: Anne Rooney
Publishing plan research and development: Reagan Miller
Project coordinator: Kathy Middleton
Photo research: Clare Hibbert
Editors: Paul Humphrey, Clare Hibbert, Rachel Eagen
Proofreader: Wendy Scavuzzo
Layout: sprout.uk.com
Illustrations: Stefan Chabluk, Discovery Picture Library, sprout.uk.com
Cover design and logo: Margaret Amy Salter
Production coordinator and prepress technician: Tammy McGarr
Print coordinator: Margaret Amy Salter

Produced for Crabtree Publishing Company by Discovery Books

Photographs:
Alamy: pp. 7 top (David Fleetham), 11 (David Preutz), 19 (dominic dibbs), 21 top (imagebroker), 21 bottom (Stephen Barnes/Technolog), 22 (ZUMA Press, Inc.), 23 (B Christopher), 24 (joefoxphoto), 25 (LJSphotography), 28 top (SCPhotos).
davekeegan.com: p. 27.
Photoshot: p. 5 (Bernd Lauter/Imagebrokers).
Shutterstock: cover (except background, top and bottom right), pp. 1 (Blend Images), 1 center-left (MariusdeGraf), 1 top-right (imagefactory), 4 (Christian Bertrand), 7 bottom (Anna Omelchenko), 9 (Tom Wang), 10 (anna karwowska), 12 (Warren Goldswain), 13 (Andi Berger), 14 (TakB), 15 top-right (Dja65), 15 center-right (Terence Mendoza), 16 (imageegami), 18 (Natursports), 20 (Mike Broglio), 27 (Elnur), 28b (lexan).
Thinkstock: cover (background and top right).
Wikimedia: Chittka L, Brockmann: cover (bottom right), pp. 17 (Cherry Yuet), 29 (NASA/JPL).

Library and Archives Canada Cataloguing in Publication

Rooney, Anne, author
Audio engineering and the science of sound waves / Anne Rooney.

(Engineering in action)
Includes index.
Issued in print and electronic formats.
ISBN 978-0-7787-1196-4 (bound).--ISBN 978-0-7787-1229-9 (pbk.).--ISBN 978-1-4271-8947-9 (pdf).--ISBN 978-1-4271-8943-1 (html)

1. Acoustical engineering--Juvenile literature. 2. Sound--Juvenile literature. 3. Sound-waves--Juvenile literature. I. Title. II. Series: Engineering in action (St. Catharines, Ont.)

TA365 R66 2013   j620.2   C2013-906143-6
C2013-906144-4

Library of Congress Cataloging-in-Publication Data

Rooney, Anne.
Audio engineering and the science of sound waves / Anne Rooney.
pages cm -- (Engineering in action)
Audience: Ages 10-13.
Audience: Grades 4 to 6.
Includes index.
ISBN 978-0-7787-1196-4 (reinforced library binding) -- ISBN 978-0-7787-1229-9 (pbk.) -- ISBN 978-1-4271-8947-9 (electronic pdf) -- ISBN (invalid) 978-1-4271-8943-1 (electronic html)
1. Sound--Recording and reproducing--Juvenile literature. 2. Acoustical engineering--Juvenile literature. I. Title.

TK7881.4.R664 2014
621.389'3--dc23
2013035439

Crabtree Publishing Company

www.crabtreebooks.com   1-800-387-7650

Printed in Canada/102013/BF20130920

Published in Canada
Crabtree Publishing
616 Welland Ave.
St. Catharines, ON
L2M 5V6

Published in the United States
Crabtree Publishing
PMB 59051
350 Fifth Avenue, 59th Floor
New York, New York 10118

Published in the United Kingdom
Crabtree Publishing
Maritime House
Basin Road North, Hove
BN41 1WR

Published in Australia
Crabtree Publishing
3 Charles Street
Coburg North
VIC, 3058

CONTENTS

What is audio engineering? 4

How sound works 6

Sound and hearing 8

Sound and radio 10

Analog and digital 12

History of audio engineering 14

Working in audio engineering 16

Starting a project 18

Trying ideas 20

First attempts 22

Refining the project 24

Design challenge: create a soundtrack 26

Into the future 28

Learning more 30

Glossary 31

Index 32

WHAT IS AUDIO ENGINEERING?

Audio engineers are people who work with sound, and the technology used to make, record, and share it. They are the magicians behind the movies, television shows, and music we enjoy.

Working with sound

You may not realize it, but you hear the work of audio engineers every day without even noticing! Sound engineers recorded your favorite songs and radio programs; they produced the soundtracks for every movie, TV show, and advertisement you've ever seen; and they designed the music and sound effects for all the computer games you've played. Audio, or sound, engineers also develop new technologies, such as voice recognition which operates devices using voice commands instead of pressing buttons.

When you enjoy a concert, you barely give a thought for all the sound engineers behind the scenes making it work!

Sound and space: Have you ever shouted inside a cave and heard an echo? Sound is affected by the space where it occurs and the materials surrounding the space. Some spaces allow sound to travel well so that a whisper can be heard across a room. Other spaces reduce sound, making noises harder to hear. *Acoustics* is the science of sound—how it is made, how it travels, and how it is heard, or received. Audio engineers are experts in acoustics.

The design process: When an audio engineer takes on a new project, he or she follows an eight-step process to design, build, and test a solution (see diagram):

SOUND, MATH, AND SCIENCE

By plucking the strings of an instrument, the ancient Greek mathematician Pythagoras noticed that shorter strings produced higher sounds, or **octaves**, while longer strings produced lower octaves. This is due to the movement, or **frequency**, of invisible sound waves. (Read more on page 6.) The relationship between sound and math is the basis of the science and engineering of sound. Science and engineering are closely linked—but are not the same thing. Scientists work to understand the world as it exists. Engineers work to shape the world to meet our needs.

Identify the problem or task

↓

Identify criteria and constraints

↓

Brainstorm possible solutions

↓

Select an approach to the problem or task

↓

Try out the approach

↓

Listen to the results → Refine the approach

↓

Share the solution

*Sound engineers use a **mixing** desk to control the volume and **balance** of different parts of the sound.*

HOW SOUND WORKS

The sounds we hear are produced by vibrations in the air called sound waves. To work with sound audio engineers need to understand how sound behaves.

Sound and molecules

Sound is carried as waves of **pressure** made by the movement of tiny particles called **molecules**. The diagram (right) shows how this works. When the bell is struck, it moves to one side. The molecules on that side are pushed together, creating an area of high pressure. When the bell swings the other way, it momentarily leaves a space in the air where it was, creating an area of low pressure called a rarefaction.

As the bell swings, waves of alternating low and high pressure radiate outward from it. Our ears detect the changes in pressure and we hear them as sound.

Sound travels in waves that are created by the movement of molecules in the air.

Sound waves can be reflected, or bounced, off a solid surface. This creates a sound repetition called an echo.

Sound waves hit the surface and travel back toward their source.

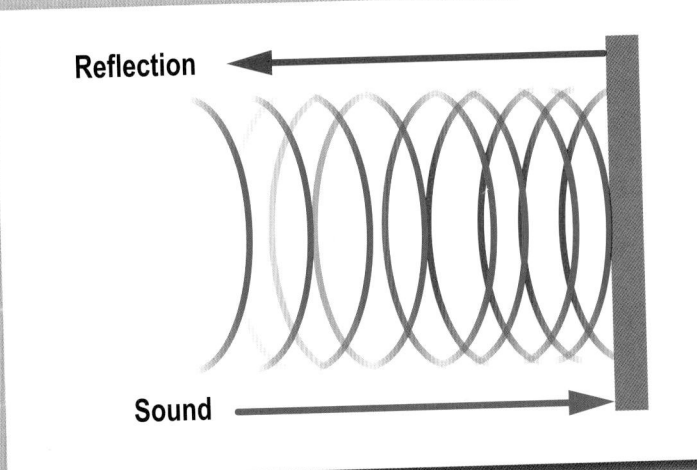

This microphone is used to record sounds under the sea. Sound waves travel more quickly through water than through air.

HOW FAST?

The first person to measure the speed of sound accurately was the British scientist and minister William Derham (1657-1735). He watched through a telescope from a church tower while a friend fired a gun 2 miles (3.2 km) away. After seeing the smoke from the fired gun, Derham counted the number of seconds it took for him to hear the shot. He found it took 9.5 seconds for the sound to travel two miles. He calculated the speed of sound through air as 1,111.6 feet per second (338.8 m/s). The actual speed of sound through dry air at 32°F (0°C) is 1,086.9 feet per second (331.3 m/s).

Silent space: Sound is carried by waves of pressure created by the movement of molecules. Sound can only move through substances with molecules, such as water, air, and solids. It cannot travel through empty space, such as a vacuum. So, if an asteroid hit the moon, we would not hear the impact since there is nothing between the moon and Earth to carry the sound waves.

In a thunderstorm, you see the lightning before you hear the thunder. That is because light travels nearly a million times faster than sound, at 186,282 miles per second (299,792 km/s).

SOUND AND HEARING

We hear by detecting the changes in air pressure that are produced by sound waves. Audio engineers also need to understand how our hearing works.

A word in your ear

Sound waves travel outward in all directions from the source of the sound. The shape of the outside of your ear, called the pinna, funnels the sound waves, which travel on air, into a tube inside your ear called the ear canal. Sound waves then hit a layer of tissue called the eardrum. On the other side of the eardrum, there is a group of tiny bones. Changes in air pressure against the eardrum move these bones. The bones **amplify** the tiny movements of the eardrum, making them 22 times stronger. Amplification—making sounds larger and louder—is an important task for audio engineers, too.

The last bone rests against the cochlea, which is a curled tube filled with liquid and about 20,000 to 30,000 tiny hairs. Vibrations move through the liquid in waves. Waves of different frequencies move hairs of different lengths. Nerves detect movement of the hairs and send an electrical signal to the brain. The brain builds the information into an idea of sound.

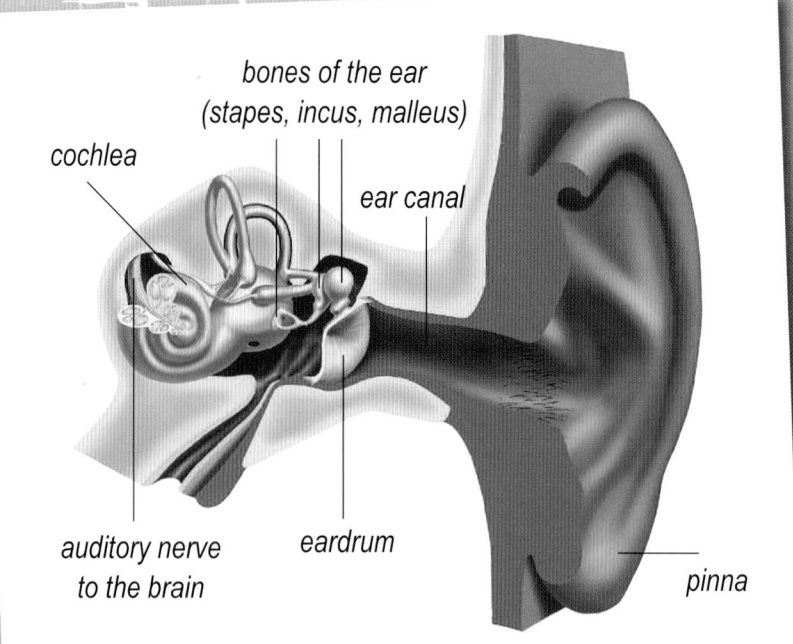

Parts of the ear

bones of the ear
(stapes, incus, malleus)

cochlea

ear canal

auditory nerve
to the brain

eardrum

pinna

PITCH AND VOLUME

A sound's *pitch* is how high or low it sounds to your ear. Your brain figures out the pitch of a sound when it receives information from hairs moving inside the cochlea. The sound's volume is determined by the number of hairs moving.

Stereo earphones can reproduce a sense of the direction that sounds come from, creating a more realistic experience than we get from a single, or mono, speaker.

Sound tricks: The fleshy outer part of the ear, or pinna, is curved. It catches the sounds and directs them to the eardrum. The way sounds are bounced off the curves of the pinna changes them slightly. We can figure out the direction a sound comes from by the differences between the sounds reaching the left and right ears. An audio engineer working on the soundtrack for a movie can control sounds in the same way to persuade us that a sound comes from a particular location in the scene.

SOUND AND RADIO

Radio, television, and cell phones transmit, or send out, sound over long distances. They do not send out sound waves, however—they send out radio waves.

Sound and light

You can't hear radio waves: they are part of the **electromagnetic spectrum**. They are waves that pass through electrical and magnetic fields. Different types of electromagnetic waves include radio, X-ray, and light. Radio waves have a long wavelength, which means they have a low frequency. The X-rays used for medical imaging have a much shorter wavelength and a higher frequency. Microwaves (like the kind used for cooking), infrared, visible light, and ultraviolet lie somewhere in between. Radio waves travel at the speed of light—nearly a million times faster than sound. Because they are energy, not waves of pressure like sound, radio waves can travel through space.

Radio waves are broadcast, or sent out in all directions, from towers called transmitters. These are often built on rooftops or high ground so they can send out the waves above other buildings.

HOW SOUND IS MEASURED

The volume of a sound is measured in decibels. The frequency of sound is the length of time between the peaks of sound waves. It is measured in hertz (Hz). One Hz is one vibration per second. Humans can hear sounds in the range 20–20,000 Hz. The pitch is determined by the frequency. A high-frequency sound has a high pitch.

Radio in and out

All broadcasts work in the same way. Sounds are converted into a pattern of electrical signals and transmitted as radio waves from an antenna.

In **analog** radio, the different sounds are transmitted as different shapes in the waves. In **digital** radio, the different sounds are transmitted in binary code (see page 13). The radio signal travels through air or space and is picked up by another antenna connected to a receiver. The receiver turns the signal back into sounds.

The cyclist's wireless earphones use radio waves to pick up transmissions from his music player or cell phone.

The shorter the distance between the peaks of sound waves, the higher the frequency. The top wave shows a lower-frequency sound than the bottom wave.

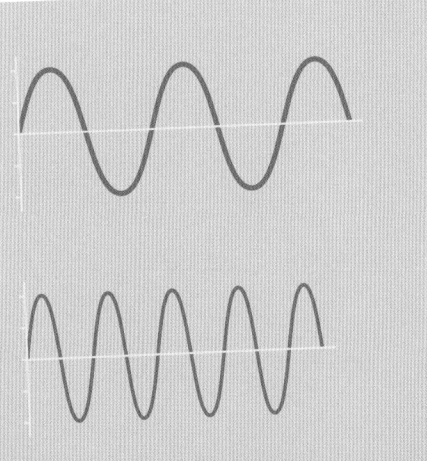

Pitch and frequency: The Italian scientist Galileo (1564-1642) was the first to show that pitch and frequency are related. He scraped a chisel over a brass plate at different speeds. The pitch of the sound varied with the speed at which he dragged the chisel.

ANALOG AND DIGITAL

Sound can be stored and transmitted in two very different ways: as an analog signal or as a digital signal.

Analog and digital data

Analog data is a continuous stream of values. An example of analog data is speed—a car doesn't leap from 30 miles per hour (48.3 km/h) to 31 miles per hour (49.9 km/h) but goes through an infinite number of speeds as it accelerates. Digital data has discrete, or definite, values. The number of people in a crowd is an example—it can only increase or decrease by units of one person, because there can't be half a person.

Analog sound

Your voice, like any other naturally occurring sound, is analog. It can vary smoothly in volume and pitch, and doesn't leap from one value to another. When your voice is recorded in analog form, all the tiny variations in the original sound can be preserved (as long as the recording mechanism is good enough). A vinyl record is an analog recording.

Vinyl records are an example of analog recordings. Their grooves store very tiny variations in sound.

Digital sound

Unlike analog sound, digital sound does leap from one value to another. It is stored as **binary** code—strings of 0s and 1s with nothing in between. The 0 and 1 can be stored, for example, as a magnetic charge on a disc or no magnetic charge. CDs and MP3 files are digital recordings.

An analog signal or recording can be shown as a continuous curve (red), but a digital signal or recording moves in steps of a whole value (gray).

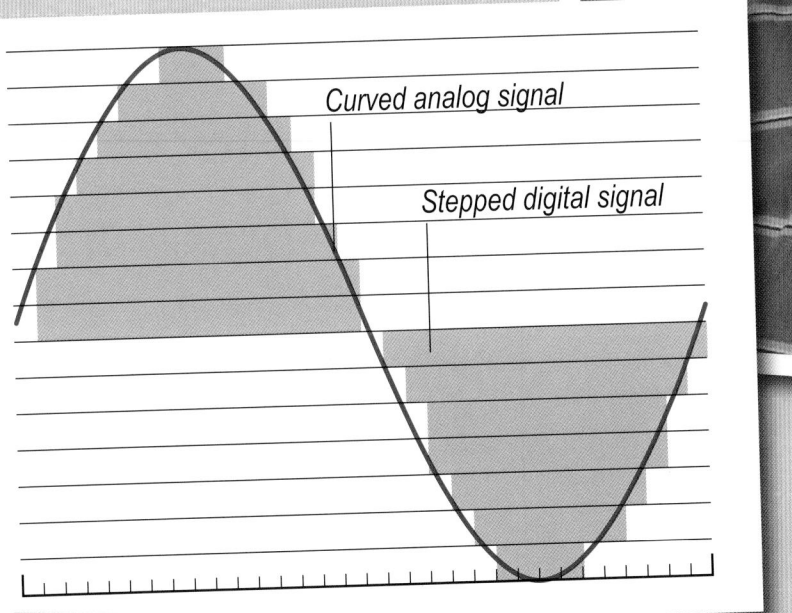

Curved analog signal

Stepped digital signal

Personal music players use digital sound recordings.

ERRORS AND DISTORTION

*Analog sound can be affected by **interference**. Because there can be slight variations, analog sound easily distorts, or changes from its true sound. Digital sound is harder to corrupt. An error has to be large enough to cause a jump to the next value. For this reason, digital sound can be completely error-free. That is hard to achieve with analog sound. On the other hand, turning analog sound into a digital signal means that the sound reproduced is only ever a close copy of the original, not an exact copy.*

HISTORY OF AUDIO ENGINEERING

Early civilizations built structures to share sound with large audiences. Their amazing discoveries shaped our understanding of acoustics today.

Built to carry sound

The ancient Greeks and Romans built oval and circular theaters called amphitheaters that had rows of seating rising one above another. Their design made the most of natural acoustics, so that the sounds of the actors' voices carried right to the very back of the seating. The stone seats helped to reflect and boost the high-frequency sounds of the voices, while cutting out low-frequency murmuring and shuffling sounds.

Built around 325 BCE, the ancient amphitheater at Epidaurus, Greece, is famous for its excellent acoustics. Performances are still put on there, and the amphitheater can seat up to 15,000 spectators.

Recording sound

Once scientists understood how sound worked, engineers began to develop methods of recording and storing sound. The first device that could record and then reproduce sounds was the phonograph, invented by Thomas Edison in 1877. It used a needle to etch a wiggly groove representing sounds onto a tinfoil-coated cylinder. When the needle moved along the groove again, the device played back the sound. The first phonographs to go on sale played cylinders coated in wax. These lasted longer than Edison's tinfoil-coated cylinder, but the wax still wore out quickly. Soon, wax cylinders were replaced with flat, hard discs called records.

Digital recording

Digital recordings such as CDs and MP3s were developed in the 1980s and 1990s. These formats allow sound to be made smaller for easy transfer and storage. Modern equipment makes it simple to record different instruments that are played at the same time onto different tracks, or channels. Afterward, they can be edited and mixed together to produce the best possible sound for a song.

The phonograph (top) could record and play back sounds spoken or played into the large, metal horn. It also played back ready-recorded sounds from hard, plastic discs. Before the use of discs, sound was recorded on wax cylinders (bottom).

FEEDBACK LOOP

Developments in audio engineering have affected the type of music created. The invention of the **synthesizer** and the development of auto-tuning—when a singer's voice is automatically corrected to perfect tones—have changed the sound of music.

WORKING IN AUDIO ENGINEERING

Audio engineers can work in many different fields and roles. Sound is important in so many areas that it's no wonder there's a big demand for audio engineers.

Areas of work

Audio engineers work in the music and film industries, in radio and television broadcasting, and at live venues such as concert halls. They can work on live and recorded sound, doing pre- and **post-production** tasks. There are also opportunities in the design of audio equipment, and restoring and digitizing old analog recordings.

Design

Sound can add to the mood, audience expectations, and setting of a play or movie. A sound designer plans the "**soundscape**"—all the sounds in a performance. The sound designer might work closely with a music composer, and decides how to use music and sound effects to achieve what the **producer** wants.

*A sound engineer works with a **soundboard** to control the sound from a live performance such as a concert or play.*

FOLEY CREWS

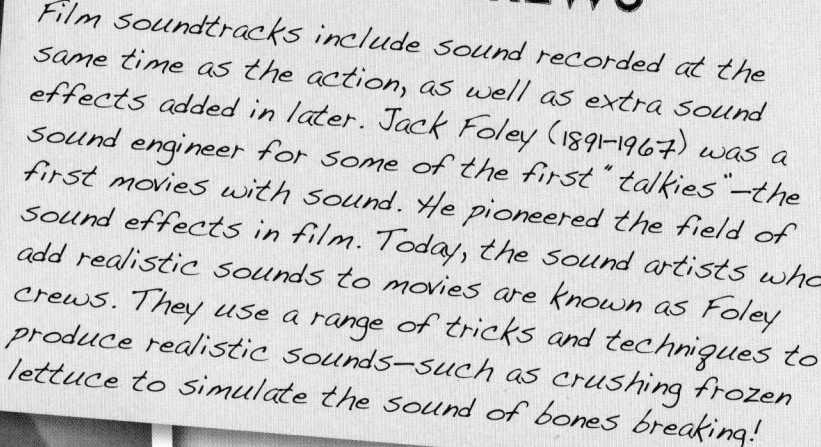

Film soundtracks include sound recorded at the same time as the action, as well as extra sound effects added in later. Jack Foley (1891-1967) was a sound engineer for some of the first "talkies"—the first movies with sound. He pioneered the field of sound effects in film. Today, the sound artists who add realistic sounds to movies are known as Foley crews. They use a range of tricks and techniques to produce realistic sounds—such as crushing frozen lettuce to simulate the sound of bones breaking!

A Foley stage has different textures set into panels and a selection of objects for the Foley crew to use to make sound effects of different types.

Recording and performance

Before a performance, an acoustic consultant advises on positions and types of equipment. Sound technicians set up the equipment and make sure it is working properly. In a recording session, a studio setup engineer is responsible for the equipment, and dismantles it afterward.

During a performance or recording, a live sound engineer or recording engineer operates the soundboard. Studio technicians are on hand to work on audio electronics.

Post-production work

Post-production engineers mix and edit tracks to create a finished product. Some audio engineers specialize in **synchronizing** sound to video, or combining sound with still or moving images, or computer games.

Skills needed: Audio engineers need a good knowledge of engineering and music technology, as well as skills in computing, math, acoustics, electronics, and physics. They have to be good at teamwork and working under pressure. Good hearing is essential.

STARTING A PROJECT

For each new project, the audio engineer has to work with others, often following direction from a producer or customer, to come up with ideas and plans.

Identify the problem or task: The first stage in an audio engineering project is to be clear about the job that needs to be done. Sometimes, a sound designer needs to advise on what will sound good. For example, a client wanting a TV ad might not know how sound creates mood and sets expectations. He or she will need guidance and suggestions from audio engineers. In other cases, the audio team will be trying to capture as perfectly as possible the sound created by an artist, or to create the effects a producer wants.

In the video-editing suite, the video and its accompanying soundtracks are put together and edited.

Selling stuff

Advertising is a huge area of business. The client often has only a very rough idea of the soundscape he or she wants. For example, an advertisement for a breakfast cereal will need upbeat, busy, early-morning sounds and lively music. Slow, relaxing sounds will not support the product. The sound engineer will work with the client's product and input to suggest suitable recording techniques and develop ideas.

Identify criteria and constraints: The second step in the engineering design process is to identify constraints. Every project has its own unique challenges and requirements. The first stage is to come up with a detailed outline that sets out the goal, what is needed, and identifies criteria and constraints.

Criteria are requirements set by the customer. Constraints are limits on the project. They can include constraints that can't be changed, such as the characteristics of the venue, or place where the event will happen. Constraints are also set by the customer, such as a budget and a project's deadline. A performance date, for example, is an immovable deadline.

Some venues, such as this racetrack, present a particular challenge. Sound engineers need to reduce background noise enough for the commentator to be heard, but keep enough to retain the exciting atmosphere.

Copyright—an important constraint: Recordings and sheet music are protected by **copyright**. That means they can't be included in a project without the permission of the copyright owner. This applies across all media. For example, you can't use a current pop song as a soundtrack to a YouTube video without permission.

TRYING IDEAS

When it's clear what is needed, the next stage is to come up with suggestions for how to carry out the project to produce what is required.

Brainstorm possible solutions: Brainstorming is a good way of starting to generate ideas for a project. Everyone involved is invited to come up with suggestions. These are written down without any criticism or evaluation. Sometimes the wackiest, most unlikely sounding ideas turn out to be the best.

Select an approach to the problem or task: When different options have been suggested, the next step is for engineers to choose one or more of the ideas to develop further and to discuss with the client. This might involve investigating technical solutions, looking at equipment or techniques, producing costings, and suggesting creative ideas to the customer.

SPECTATOR SPORTS

Many sports events are broadcast live from outdoor venues. Before an outside broadcast, such as coverage of a lacrosse game, the broadcasting team can visit the venue, examine conditions, and anticipate any problems. They can try recording in different spots using various types of microphones. They can judge the levels of ambient, or background, noise and choose suitable techniques and equipment, such as the right microphones. They might also plan for unexpected conditions on the event day—such as loud wind or noise from passing aircraft—that will need different sound recording and mixing techniques.

There are two jobs for sound engineers at a big lacrosse game: setting up a sound system so the crowd can hear the scores, and helping to broadcast the event for radio and TV.

Getting it right

Although post-production work can improve a recording, it's very important to make the right choices before recording a live performance. For example, choosing inappropriate types of microphones or putting them in the wrong positions are errors that can't be corrected after the recording and can destroy a performance. The choice and setup of a public address (**PA**) system for a live performance sets limits on how it will sound before an artist even arrives. The audio engineers need to know what effects their choices will have on the quality of the sound.

Sound engineers set up and check the sound system at a conference center in Switzerland.

A sound engineer works with portable equipment while filming on location, or not in a studio. There will be the opportunity to do a lot of post-production work, but it's important to have the right sounds to work with.

FIRST ATTEMPTS

After choosing a solution and developing it, audio engineers present it to the client for discussion and feedback. This could involve choosing the PA system that will be used for a live event or playing back first recordings to a band.

Try out the approach: The next stage is to try out the idea, which could mean deciding which tracks to use to build up the finished soundtrack. For example, a movie has several separately recorded voice, special effects, and music tracks. A band will record each instrument and singer onto different tracks. For example, each guitar will have a magnetic **pickup** that converts the sound from the guitar to an electric signal, which is amplified and recorded as a single track. There will be several microphones placed around a drum kit. All tracks are recorded at the same time while the band plays, and can be processed and edited separately after the recording. The band can make several recordings of all or part of a song at different times—in different studios or even countries—then build the best combination from the various recordings.

Sound engineers put together the final version of the song in a post-production suite, or studio.

Listening and playing

As soon as some tracks have been recorded, they can be played back and used during another recording. So a singer can listen to three or four instrumental tracks while recording vocals, for example.

Listen to the results:
The next step in the process is to listen to the results. An audio engineer compares different recordings of the same track and uses the best parts from each.

WORKING TOGETHER

Often, several people are involved in the development of a project, and everyone has to be prepared to accept changes to their plans and ideas. Parts of the project might have to be adjusted to fit the needs of other aspects. For example, a plan for the sound system for an awards ceremony will have to fit the layout of the venue and work with the script used by the presenters. The choice of pickup will have to suit the style of guitar an artist uses.

At a live performance, the sound engineer controls the mix or sounds as they come in from the pickups and microphones on different instruments and singers.

REFINING THE PROJECT

Once the recording engineer has finished work, the mixing engineers take over. The sound for a movie or album goes through a lot of post-production work that involves editing, mixing, and remixing.

Refine the approach: The final soundtrack is put together by combining the best parts from various recordings and adding any extra effects to change the quality of the sound. An audio engineer uses a mixing board to do this. He or she may go back and rerecord some of the tracks if they haven't turned out quite right.

Building a soundtrack

Today, audio engineers use editing techniques that do not change the original sound files. Instead, an edit decision list (EDL) file stores the changes and choices that are applied to copies of the files. The sound editor can go directly to any part of the recording and use techniques such as cut-and-paste to move sections between tracks.

UNPICKING SOUND

Not all sound engineers work to build up sounds—some take them apart. In forensic work, audio engineers work with recordings that are often poor quality to retrieve evidence or analyze the sound. They might reduce background noise from a recorded phone conversation or tape to pinpoint each voice so they can be analyzed by a voice expert. Alternatively they may boost a background sound that contains valuable information, such as the sound of a crime being committed.

Forensic experts can boost external noise to try to find out the circumstances or location in which a phone call was made.

Final production

The mixing engineer "mixes down," or combines, tracks as they are perfected. When the mixing engineer has finished work, a mastering engineer adds finishing touches to the mix, such as equalization, overall effects, and perhaps **compression**. Equalization involves smoothing out the variation in frequencies to cut out hiss, interference, and imbalance between instruments or voices to produce a more even sound. Effects change how sounds are played back. For example, adding reverberation makes a sound continue, as though echoing around a room after the sound-making source has stopped. Compression turns down louder sounds and boosts quieter sounds.

Three microphones around the drum kit let the sound engineer choose or switch between three drum tracks after the recording has been made.

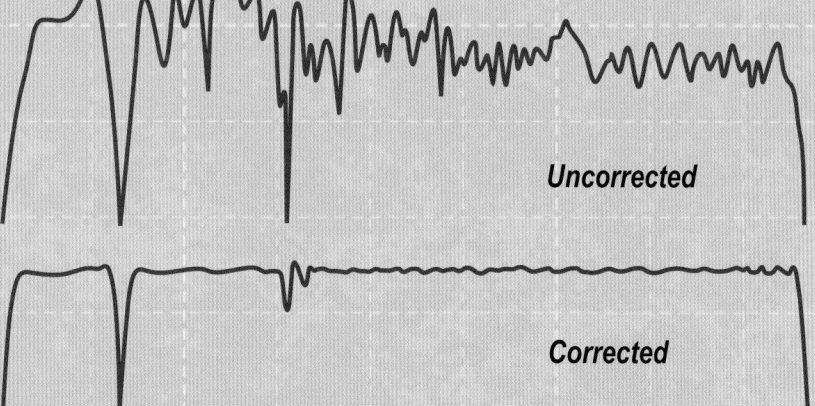

Uncorrected

Corrected

The corrected sound is much smoother, with disturbance removed. The smoother wave pattern shows this.

Share your results: When the mixing engineer is happy with the end result, the sound can be shared. If it's music for an album, that album can go on sale to the public. If it's the soundtrack for a movie, it will be heard when the movie is released.

DESIGN CHALLENGE: CREATE A SOUNDTRACK

The best way to understand some of the processes involved in audio engineering is to try it yourself. There is lots of software available for mixing and editing sounds.

1: The problem: Your task is to add a soundtrack to a short video clip.

2: Requirements and constraints: Do you want to make something lively, funny, relaxing, thoughtful, or sad? Can you make your own video and record your own sound? Does your school have equipment you could use?

3: Brainstorm!: Find or make a video clip. Figure out which music you could use and, if making your own video, decide whether you will record a **voiceover** or live sound. Will you add any special sound effects?

4: Choose a solution: Decide which of your ideas best matches the goals you set. Have you picked the right music for the mood you want? Can you make the sound effects you need? Make sure everything you need is available and record any sounds that you need.

5: First attempt: If you don't have access to editing software, you can record whole tracks onto a CD. If you are able to use software, you will be able to see the different tracks as separate items onscreen. When do you want them to start, stop, and restart? Would you like any of the tracks to overlap? As the audio engineer, you get to choose!

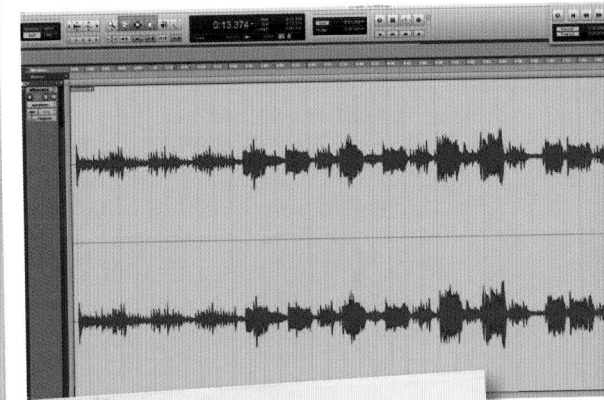

6: Test your first attempt: Play back the video with its soundtrack. Does it do what you want? What should you change? Do you need different music, voiceover, or special effects?

7: Improve your work: Edit individual sound clips to change their volume, balance, or other features. Listen to all your changes and make sure you can tell how the track sounds different. Remember to save your work frequently.

Will you record your own music for the soundtrack? Or will you use recordings by other artists?

8: Share your results: When you are happy with how the sound and video tracks work together, create a finished video file. Play it to your family and friends and ask them what they think.

INTO THE FUTURE

Developments in audio engineering technologies mean that more young musicians can experiment with editing and mixing their own music. At the same time, there are more unusual applications of some of the techniques audio engineers use, which is opening up new areas of work.

Sound archives

Recording sound has been around for about 150 years. Old recordings use old technology and are of poor quality. They also degrade, or break down, further over time. In sound **archiving** and restoration, digital remastering engineers create digital files from old records and analog tapes, cleaning up distortion and errors, and preserving the sound for the future.

Speak to your car

Voice-recognition and voice-activation systems are increasingly used. Sound engineers work with computer programmers and language experts to gather and process voice instructions and turn them into instructions a computer can understand. One of the most exciting developments is the voice-operated car, the Lexus 2008. Voice-activated equipment is especially helpful for people with physical disabilities.

Sound engineers test equipment designed to block out noise. People who work with loud equipment, such as construction workers, use noise-blocking headphones to protect their hearing.

The voice commands recognized by the Lexus 2008 include instructions to go to stored destinations, show facilities (such as hospitals and restaurants) on the map, and control the heating and sound systems.

Voices into space:
The two spacecraft, Voyager 1 and 2, launched in 1977, carry Golden Records that include sounds from Earth. The spacecraft also carry diagrams that show how to play the gold-plated copper discs. Simple sound engineering from Earth is now speeding out of the solar system in search of alien listeners!

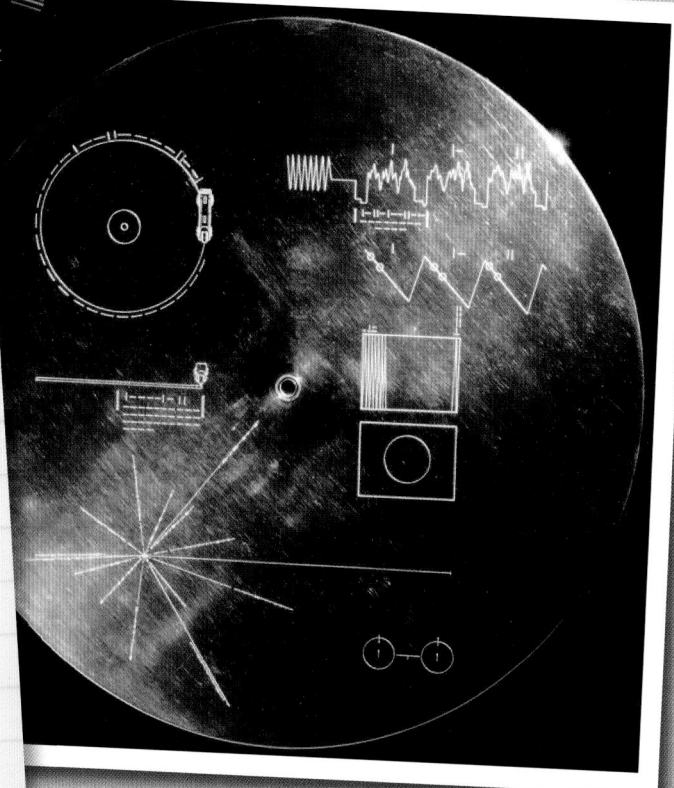

The Golden Records on the Voyager spacecraft can be played with simple equipment anywhere in space. Voyager 1 will not pass near another star for 40,000 years.

SOUND FROM PAPER

In 2012, researchers at Indiana University produced a sound file from a photograph of an old phonograph record. They straightened out the image of the long groove in the record, filled any gaps, used software to convert the line to a digital file, and then played the sound. The oldest sound recording restored from paper dates from 1877.

LEARNING MORE

BOOKS

Judith Anderson, *Behind the Scenes: Music*, Wayland, 2009

Matthew Anniss, *The Music Scene: The Music Industry*, Franklin Watts, 2012

Sarah Medina, *Behind the Scenes: Television*, Wayland, 2013

Mike Senior, *Mixing Secrets for the Small Studio*, Focal Press, 2011

Tania Shillam, *Careers Uncovered: Music Industry*, Trotman Publishing, 2007

Richard Spilsbury, *I'm Good at Music: What Job Can I Get?*, Wayland, 2013

ONLINE

www.berklee.edu/careers/mpe
Information about the many different careers in audio engineering.

www.exploresound.org
All about acoustics, with facts, fun games, and loads of resources.

www.youtube.com/watch?v=_ovMh2A3P5k
A video demonstrating how sound works and how it travels through air.

PLACES TO VISIT

Museum of the Moving Image, New York, USA: www.movingimage.us

www.thestudiotour.com has information about studios you can tour, such as Warner Brothers, Paramount, Sony, and Universal in Los Angeles, California, and BBC Television Centre in London, UK.

www.bbc.co.uk/news/magazine-20773690 lists places in Britain with unusual sound properties: St Paul's Cathedral, London; the anechoic chamber at the University of Salford; Greenwich Foot Tunnel, London; Wormit Reservoir, Dundee.

GLOSSARY

acoustics The science of investigating, understanding, and producing sound

amplify To make larger or louder

analog Describes a form of data that can have a continual range of values

archiving Placing something in an archive—a store of old materials or data kept for its historical value

balance The volume level relationship between musical elements

binary Capable of existing in only two states or values

compression The lessening of the range between the loudest and quietest parts of an audio signal

copyright Property rights that protect the ownership of artistic creations, such as music, videos, and books

digital Describes a form of data that can only exist in whole discrete values

electromagnetic spectrum The range of forms of energy that exist as waves in electric and magnetic fields, including light, radio, and X-rays

forensic Describes the use of science to solve crime

frequency The interval between the peaks and troughs in a sound wave, measured as waves per second (hertz)

interference Problems caused by sound waves running into and over each other

mixing Combining the best parts from various recordings and adding any extra effects to change the quality of the sound

molecules The smallest components of particular types of matter, made up of atoms

octaves Ranges of eight notes between one musical pitch and another that have double or half its frequency

PA Public address system—the equipment used to relay sound in a performance

pickup A piece of equipment that 'picks up' sounds, converts them to electrical signals, and relays them to recording or broadcasting equipment

pitch How high or low a note sounds

post-production Carried out after sounds have been recorded

pressure The action of a force against another force

producer The person in charge of the overall creation and design of a production (video, recording, or performance)

soundboard The mixing desk or console used by sound engineers to control how the sounds produced by performers are broadcast or recorded

soundscape All the sounds, such as voice, music, and sound effects, in a production

synchronizing Making things happen at the same time, for example, making the sound of a voice match lip movements in a movie

synthesizer An electric instrument that produces sounds that mimic those of other instruments and create synthetic sounds

voiceover The voice track laid over a video to provide a commentary or other information

INDEX

acoustics 4, 14, 17
advertisements 4, 18
amphitheaters 14
amplification 8, 20, 22
analog sound 11, 12–13, 16, 28
archiving 28

brainstorming 5, 20

computer games 4, 17
concerts 4, 16

decibels 10
Derham, William 7
design process 5, 18, 19, 20, 22, 23, 24, 25
digital sound 11, 12–13, 15, 28
distortion 13, 28

echoes 4, 6, 25
Edison, Thomas 15
electromagnetic spectrum 10

Foley crews 17
forensic experts 24
frequency 5, 8, 10, 11, 14, 25

Galileo 11
Golden Records 29

hearing 4, 6, 7, 8, 10, 14, 17, 19, 28
hertz 10

mixing 5, 15, 17, 20, 23, 24–25, 26, 28
movies 4, 9, 16, 17, 22, 24

octaves 5

phonographs 15, 29
pitch 9, 10, 11, 12
post-production 16, 17, 21, 22, 24
producers 16, 18
Pythagoras 5

radio 4, 10–11, 20
restoration 28

sound waves 6–7, 8, 10, 11
soundscapes 16, 18
soundtracks 4, 9, 17, 18, 19, 22, 24, 26–27
speed of sound 7
sports events 19, 20
stereo sound 9

television 4, 10, 18, 20
transmitters 10

video editing 18, 27
vinyl records 12
voice recognition 4, 28
voice-activation systems 28
voiceovers 26, 27
volume 5, 9, 10, 12, 27

wax cylinders 15